WARS OF SOUTH AMERICAN INDEPENDENCE

A History from Beginning to End

Copyright © 2019 by Hourly History.

All rights reserved.

Table of Contents

Introduction
Background
The Succession Crisis
William Wallace's War
Robert the Bruce
An Uneasy Peace
The Pretender to the Throne
Return of the King
The End of the Wars
Aftermath
Conclusion

Introduction

The United Kingdom was not always united. England, Wales, Northern Ireland, and Scotland were at various times during their history sovereign and independent nations. By the late thirteenth century, England had become the most powerful of all the British nations. England controlled not just Ireland and Wales but also parts of northern France. All that remained was for Scotland to be brought under English control.

This led to two separate wars which continued into the second half of the fourteenth century. These conflicts saw the emergence of two of Scotland's best-known national heroes—William Wallace and Robert the Bruce—and led to Scotland asserting itself as an independent nation. These wars also introduced new tactics and new weapons in medieval warfare, which would transform conflict not just in Britain but across Europe.

These conflicts are now known as the Wars of Scottish Independence (though they were not given this name until much later, following the American Revolutionary War), but the causes of these wars are complex with an array of characters whose motives are not always transparent or related directly to the struggle for Scottish independence. The conflicts themselves are also complicated with a whole series of battles, some conclusive, most not, some large and some small, which favored first one side and then the other before finally leading to a conclusion.

This is the convoluted and sometimes heroic story of the Wars of Scottish Independence.

Chapter One

Background

"Where is the coward that would not dare to fight for such a land as Scotland?"

—Sir Walter Scott

The story of the Wars of Scottish Independence begins in the mid-1200s. The map of the British Isles looked very different then. Wales was not a separate country but a principality ruled by England after centuries of bitter conflict. Most of Ireland was also controlled by England, but to the north, Scotland was a separate country with a border agreed in the Treaty of York in 1237 which ran from Carlisle in the west to Berwick in the east. The Norman invasion of England less than 200 years before had meant that England also controlled lands in the north of present-day France, known as the Angevin Empire. French was the language spoken in the English court and used by English kings, diplomats, and politicians.

As a legacy of the Viking invasions, many of the islands surrounding Britain were still controlled by Norway at that time, including Orkney, Shetland, the Western Isles, and the Isle of Man. Although Scotland and England were separate countries, there were a number of family and other connections between them—King Alexander II of Scotland, who ruled from 1214-1249, was also created a knight of the English court by King John, for example. There had been a long period of peace between Scotland and England in the thirteenth century though there had been frequent conflicts in the past. The circumstances which led to the Wars of Scottish Independence included a series of accidents and the ascension to power of ambitious and aggressive men.

When Alexander II of Scotland died in July of 1249, his son and heir, Alexander III, was just seven years old. Until he reached the age of 21, Scotland would be ruled by a regency of guardians and this led to the emergence of two separate groups, one led by Walter Comyn, the earl of Menteith, and the other by Alan Durward, the justiciar of Scotia. These two powerful groups would compete for control of Scotland until the new king reached the age of majority.

In 1251, a marriage was arranged between the ten-year-old Alexander and Margaret, daughter of King Henry III of England. Henry III was an astute and pious king who hoped to use this alliance to make Scotland a fiefdom of England, but at a meeting between the kings, Alexander refused.

As soon as he attained his majority in 1262, Alexander announced that he would begin a campaign to re-take the Western Isles and the Isle of Man for Scotland. He made a formal claim to King Haakon of Norway, but this was refused and the Norwegian king sent an invasion fleet to Scotland. This fleet was anchored off the Island of Arran while negotiations continued, and Alexander was able to prolong the discussions until autumn storms ravaged the fleet which then returned to Norway after a short and indecisive battle. Haakon died soon after, and his successor agreed to the ceding of the Western Isles and the Isle of Man to Scotland in exchange for a large payment, though Orkney and Shetland would continue to be part of Norway until 1469.

By 1284, the position between Scotland and England was relatively settled, and Alexander III had proven to be a moderate and effective leader. However, the question of who would succeed him was becoming a pressing issue. Queen Margaret died in 1275 after bearing the king three children: a daughter and two sons. The daughter, Margaret, had married King Eric II of Norway but died in childbirth in 1283. Both Alexander's sons had died by 1284 and neither had left children. The issue of an heir was not thought to be pressing—after all, the king was only 43, and in November 1285, he married for the second time, to Frenchwoman Yolande de Dreux. It was expected that the king would produce new heirs through this marriage, but in the meantime, Alexander named as his heir his only grandchild, Margaret, known as the Maid of Norway, who had survived her mother's death in 1283.

It soon became apparent that the new queen of Scotland was pregnant, and it seemed that the succession was safe. Then, in March 1286, Alexander decided to travel from Edinburgh Castle to visit his queen at her residence in Kinghorn in Fife to be with her for her birthday the following day. The weather was bad, and it was late afternoon before the king was ready to set off. He was advised not to undertake the trip but set off anyway. He failed to arrive in Kinghorn, and a search the following morning discovered the king's body at the bottom of a steep, rocky escarpment. It seemed that his horse must have stumbled in the darkness, and the king had broken his neck. Suddenly, the question of who would become the next ruler of Scotland was much more pressing.

Chapter Two

The Succession Crisis

"This is my country,

The land that begat me."

—Sir Alexander Gray

Although Alexander III had nominated the Maid of Norway as his heir, there was hope that if Yolande de Dreux produced a child, this would automatically become the next ruler of Scotland. It was also clear that, as the Maid of Norway was just three years old, a regency of guardians would be required to rule until the new monarch reached the age of majority. At a gathering of Scottish nobles, a regency of six guardians, known as the Guardians of Scotland, were elected. The question of the succession was settled when Yolande de Dreux's child by King Alexander was stillborn—the Maid of Norway was to be the next ruler of Scotland.

Not everyone was content with this situation. Robert Bruce, a Scottish nobleman and the grandfather of Robert the Bruce, objected, and a conflict broke out between his forces and those of the Guardians. Robert Bruce was defeated in battle in 1287, but King Eric of Norway was reluctant to send his three-year-old daughter into what appeared to be a volatile and potentially dangerous situation in Scotland. He appealed to King Edward I of England for help. Edward, sensing an opportunity to increase English influence in Scotland, agreed. Margaret was to be sent to England, where she would receive the protection of Edward. She would not be sent to Scotland until he deemed it safe. Edward also negotiated the right to choose the new queen's future husband.

Reassured, King Eric agreed for his daughter to leave Norway. On September 23, 1290, the ship carrying Margaret to England called in at the Norwegian territory of Orkney. The young girl had become ill on the journey, though no-one was certain whether this was sea-sickness caused by the rough crossing or something more serious. A few days later, she was dead. Suddenly, the question of who would rule Scotland was once again a matter of importance—and confusion.

With the death of Margaret, the line which had descended directly from King William I of Scotland was broken. Instead, a new line from his son, David, the earl of Huntingdon, took precedence. Unfortunately, this produced two men with equally powerful claims to the throne. John Balliol was the grandson of the eldest daughter of the earl of Huntingdon. His main rival was the rebellious Robert Bruce, the son of the earl's second daughter. Balliol's claim was based on the principle of primogeniture, the right by custom of the firstborn legitimate son to inherit an entire estate—Balliol was the relative of the eldest of Huntingdon's daughters. Bruce, however, claimed with some justification that he was the closest claimant in terms of blood relationship, being one step closer to the earl of Huntingdon than Balliol.

Both men gathered support, and it looked as if Scotland was headed for civil war. In desperation, the Guardians of Scotland turned to Edward I to adjudicate the dispute. Edward again recognized an opportunity to increase English influence over Scotland. He invited the Scots to attend a meeting at Norham Castle, close to the border but in land claimed by England. The Scots declined, fearing that such a meeting would give the appearance of Scotland accepting the rule of England. Edward then demanded that, if he was to mediate between the rival claimants, Scotland must be willing to accept that it was subject to the rule of England. This too was rejected.

Desperate to become king, first Robert Bruce and then John Balliol traveled to England to meet with Edward and to offer homage. Both accepted Edward's claim to the title lord paramount of Scotland. Edward then knew that whichever claimant he chose, they would have to accept some measure of English control. In 1292, Edward announced that he had reached a decision: John Balliol was the rightful king of Scotland, and at a ceremony later that year in Berwick, he was crowned King John of Scotland. In exchange for the support of Edward, Balliol had promised the English king greater influence in Scottish affairs. Edward was given control over every royal castle in Scotland, and every Scottish official was required to resign his post before being re-appointed by Edward in a ceremony in which all were required to acknowledge the English king as lord paramount of Scotland. These measures caused dissent in Scotland, and worse was to follow.

Edward had inherited control over the dukedom of Aquitaine in northern France. Through the Treaty of Paris in 1259, peace had finally been assured between France and England, but it was clear to most people that this was only a temporary state of affairs. English control of northern France extended back to the eleventh century when King William was also the duke of Normandy. England looked to expand the territory it controlled in France while France wished to expel the English completely from mainland Europe. Edward built up a formidable army, but this was expensive to maintain. Soon he was demanding taxes from Scotland to contribute to these costs and Scottish troops to bolster his army. In 1294, Edward summoned King John to England and instructed him that he was to provide troops and finance to support a planned English invasion of France.

When John returned to Scotland, it was clear that there was no popular support for these actions, and instead, Scotland began secret negotiations with France. It was agreed that, in the event of an English invasion of France, Scotland would attack England and that if England invaded Scotland, France would attack England. The agreement was confirmed with an arrangement for King John's son, Edward, to marry Joan, the niece of King Philip IV of France. This secret alliance, often referred to in Scotland as the Auld Alliance, would remain in effect for more than 200 years.

In the summer of 1295, King Edward became aware of the terms of the secret treaty. He was extremely angry—not only were the Scots failing to provide the funds and troops he badly needed, they were siding with England's archenemy, France. This put England in a difficult position with the potential of facing a war on two fronts. This was something that Edward realized he could not hope to win, and he decided that he would have to deal with the Scots before turning his attention to France. Edward began sending troops to the Scottish border and strengthened his defenses there. King John responded by calling up all able-bodied men to join the Scottish armies, and by early 1296, the two forces faced each other across the border. It seemed to most people that a war between Scotland and England was now inevitable.

Chapter Three

William Wallace's War

"We come here with no peaceful intent, but ready for battle, determined to avenge our wrongs and set our country free. Let your masters come and attack us: we are ready to meet them beard to beard."

—William Wallace

By the late thirteenth century, the Scottish city of Berwick-upon-Tweed, close to the English border, was one of the most prosperous and important of all British cities. Trade between Scotland and England as well as through other European ports brought great wealth to the city, and by 1295, it was the second most important city in Britain after London. An English bishop of the period described the city as "populous and of such commercial importance that it might rightly be called another Alexandria." When Edward had made the proclamation announcing that John Balliol was to be the next king of Scotland, this was done in the Great Hall of Berwick Castle.

Yet its position close to the border made Berwick vulnerable, and when Edward launched an invasion of Scotland in March 1296, his first target was the city of Berwick. Despite its defenses, the city quickly fell to the English. Medieval warfare was brutally violent with the massacre of civilians and non-combatants commonplace, but the sack of Berwick that followed its capture was extreme even by contemporary standards. An account written soon after noted that "Edward spared no one, whatever the age or sex, and for two days streams of blood flowed from the bodies of the slain, for in his tyrannous rage he ordered 7,500 souls of both sexes to be massacred . . . So that mills could be turned by the flow of their blood." It has been estimated that as many as 20,000 civilians may have been killed at Berwick.

On April 5, 1296, while he was still in Berwick, Edward received a message from King John of Scotland, formally renouncing his oath of homage to the English king. Edward's response was recorded as, "O' foolish knave! What folly he commits. If he will not come to us we will go to him." On April 27, relatively small English and Scots armies clashed near Dunbar Castle, a few miles north of Berwick. The result was a complete defeat of the Scottish army and, though no-one quite realized it at the time, the end of the first phase of the Wars of Scottish Independence. Defeat at the Battle of Dunbar effectively ended Scottish military resistance to the English invasion. Important Scottish castles at Roxburgh, Edinburgh, and Stirling either surrendered or quickly fell to the English. By the end of June 1296, organized resistance was at an end, and King John agreed to surrender.

In early July, John confessed to rebellion and asked King Edward for forgiveness. He renounced the treaty with France, and in a ceremony on July 8, he was formally stripped of the vestments of kingship. This included having the coat of arms of Scotland torn from his surcoat by the bishop of Durham. This led to the contemptuous nickname by which John became known to many Scots—Toom Tabard ("the empty coat"). John and his son were taken to England and into captivity. King Edward appropriated important symbols of Scottish national identity, including the Stone of Scone (the stone on which Scottish kings were traditionally crowned), and took them back to England. As he left Scotland, Edward was heard to remark, "A man does good work when he rids himself of s--t." It seemed to most people that the War for Scottish Independence was over. In fact, it was only just beginning.

Many Scots chafed at what amounted to English occupation, and several Scottish nobles led rebellions against English rule. Two of the most successful were Andrew Moray, the lord of extensive estates in northeastern Scotland, and a man who would go on to become one of Scotland's best-known national heroes, William Wallace. The early history of Wallace is largely unknown and still disputed—he is thought to have been the son of a Scottish feudal lord in either Renfrewshire or Ayrshire, and his subsequent military success strongly suggests that he had some experience of battle, though no-one is certain where this took place.

What is known is that Wallace was behind the assassination in May 1297 of William de Heselrig, the English-appointed high sheriff of Lanark. Wallace then set up a base of operations in Ettrick Forest in the south of Scotland from where he and his men conducted a number of successful raids against small English positions. Although some rebellious Scottish lords surrendered to the English in July 1297, Wallace in the south and Moray in the north continued to fight. At some point in the summer of 1297, the two men met and combined their forces, and soon they controlled most of Scotland beyond Stirling. In response, King Edward sent a large army under the command of John de Warenne, the 6th earl of Surrey, to crush the new rebellion. On September 11, 1297, the English army met the combined forces of Wallace and Moray in battle at a small wooden bridge over the River Forth near Stirling Castle.

On paper, the outcome looked certain. Medieval warfare focused on heavily armored mounted troops on large armored horses, and these knights became an icon for what has become known as the Age of Chivalry. They were supported by armored foot soldiers, the men-at-arms, and large numbers of more lightly armored infantry armed with weapons such as spears. The English army was experienced, well-equipped, and most importantly included around 2,000 heavy cavalry supported by around 7,000 infantry. The Scottish army was mainly infantry, with around 5,000 foot soldiers, but these were not as well-equipped or armored as their English counterparts. In addition, the Scots had only around 300 cavalry—a major disadvantage against the English force which included much larger numbers of mounted knights. These heavy cavalry were the tanks of medieval warfare, heavily armored shock troops used to smash through enemy lines. The preponderance of these troops on the English side seemed to make an English victory certain, and anyway, no Scottish army had defeated the English for hundreds of years.

The outcome was very different. The Scots cut off a large part of the English army once it had crossed the narrow, wooden bridge and effectively destroyed it. The earl of Surrey panicked and withdrew from the field, leaving behind almost 5,000 English dead and effectively handing control of the Lowlands to the Scots.

Andrew Moray was grievously wounded during the battle and died soon after, leaving William Wallace as the single leader of the Scottish army. Wallace was appointed as Guardian of Scotland and went on to lead a series of raids into the north of England, which prompted King Edward to march north again with his army in 1298. Wallace and Edward finally met in battle at Falkirk on July 22, 1298. Once again, the English army was larger, approximately 15,000 opposed by 6,000 Scots. However, this time, the English infantry included large numbers of longbowmen.

The longbow was a devastating weapon. Only the English army included these troops, and the heavy arrows fired from these large bows could penetrate armor and shields. Other armies included crossbowmen, but while these were also effective, they could not match the rate of fire provided by trained longbowmen. It took anything up to one minute to reload a crossbow while an experienced longbowman could shoot up to 14 arrows per minute. Longbowmen shot so quickly that they could have several arrows in the air before the first had landed on its target. When massed formations of longbowmen released a volley of arrows, it had a devastating effect on the enemy. It wasn't until the appearance of firearms on the battlefield in the early 1400s that the longbow declined in importance as a military weapon.

The Scottish infantry, still mainly comprising spearmen, formed into tightly-packed formations known as schiltrons. These provided excellent defense against heavy cavalry attack, but they were also ideal targets for the English longbowmen. The English army stood back, using formations of men-at-arms to protect their archers while the longbowmen rained a deadly hail of arrows on the Scottish formations. This was a new tactic in medieval warfare, and its effect was devastating. The Scottish schiltrons were virtually destroyed by the constant rain of arrows, and when Edward sent his cavalry and infantry in to finish the job, all they had to do was mop up the survivors. Those who could fled into the nearby forest of Torwood.

William Wallace escaped after the battle, although precisely what happened to him in the years that followed is unclear. It has been suggested that he went to France as an envoy for Scotland and that perhaps he even fought on the side of the French who were by that time also involved in a series of skirmishes with England. The friction with the French forced Edward to curtail his subjugation of Scotland and to return to the south to focus on that conflict.

Chapter Four

Robert the Bruce

"We fight not for glory, nor for wealth, nor honour but only and alone for freedom which no good man surrenders but with his life."

—Robert the Bruce

After the disastrous defeat at the Battle of Falkirk, William Wallace lost both his reputation as an astute military tactician and the confidence of his men. He left Scotland, most likely to travel to France though that is not certain, and in December 1298, he resigned as Guardian of Scotland. No one other man was sufficiently dominant within the Scottish forces to take his place, and instead two men were given the positions of Guardians of Scotland.

Robert the Bruce, the earl of Carrick, was the grandson of Robert Bruce who had been a claimant to the throne and lost in the contest against John Balliol. The Bruce family had never given up their claim to be the true kings of Scotland, but they had fared badly while King John ruled. The situation was made worse for the Bruce family because many of King John's closest advisors at court were members of their most bitter enemies, the Comyn family.

When war had broken out between Scottish rebels and the forces of King Edward in 1296, the Bruce family had initially sided with Edward. Members of the Bruce family had been amongst more than 1,000 Scottish nobles who gathered at Berwick to swear an oath of fealty to King Edward in August of 1296. However, when the Scottish rebellion re-ignited in 1297, it was joined by the 22-year-old Robert the Bruce, seemingly against the wishes of his father. He told his men: "No man holds his own flesh and blood in hatred and I am no exception. I must join my own people and the nation in which I was born."

By 1298, Robert the Bruce had become such an important factor in the Scottish rebellion that he was appointed Guardian of Scotland. A second Guardian was also appointed: John Comyn, a nephew of the deposed King John and a man who also had a legitimate claim on the Scottish throne. The two men seem to have hated one another, and their continuing enmity was so great that, in 1299, the bishop of St. Andrews was appointed as a third, neutral, Guardian whose role was to try and prevent friction between the other two. This did not work, and the Scottish nobles became divided into Bruce and Comyn factions. In 1301, all three Guardians resigned and Sir John de Soules was appointed as sole Guardian. He was chosen principally because he was not a part of either faction, and he attempted to reconcile both while continuing efforts to have John returned to the throne.

During this period, King Edward continued in his efforts to crush the Scots. In 1301, he launched his sixth invasion of Scotland but, though English troops occupied parts of the south of Scotland, this produced no decisive result. In 1302, Edward offered a nine-month truce, and Robert the Bruce, with other Scottish nobles, surrendered to the English king. It wasn't until yet another invasion in

1304 that Edward was able to bring most of Scotland under English control. By February 1304, William Wallace was the only notable Scottish noble who had not surrendered to the English. When he was captured and executed in 1305, it seemed that Scottish resistance to English rule was at an end.

Robert the Bruce remained one of the most powerful Scottish nobles and one of the leading contenders for the Scottish throne. His main rival was still John Comyn who, because he had been much more determined in fighting the English, maintained a large following in Scotland. It is claimed, however, that Bruce and Comyn had concluded a secret agreement whereby Comyn would give up his claim to the throne in exchange for the support of Bruce and his followers in another insurrection against English rule.

It seems that King Edward discovered the details of this agreement and Bruce, who was at that time attending the English court in London, was forced to flee back to Scotland. Bruce and Comyn agreed to a clandestine meeting in the chapel of Greyfriars Monastery in Dumfries in February of 1306. Precisely what happened that day is a matter of dispute, but it seems that Bruce accused Comyn of treachery and blows were exchanged. Weapons were drawn and John Comyn was killed. Bruce was now the undisputed claimant to the Scottish throne.

In March 1306, just six weeks after the death of John Comyn, Robert the Bruce was crowned king of Scotland by Bishop William de Lamberton at Scone, near Perth. Bruce immediately began to gather an army with which to face the English. His first military engagement as king was a disaster. Edward sent an army north, and the Scots under the command of Bruce were heavily defeated at the Battle of Methven in June. Bruce fled from the battlefield with a small group of men and was almost killed when his force was ambushed by members of the MacDougall and MacNab clans led by John MacDougall, a kinsman of the murdered John Comyn. Bruce escaped and went into hiding in the west of Scotland. During this period, his brother Neil was captured by the English and executed, and his wife and sisters, Mary and Christina, were hung in cages at castles controlled by the English.

It seemed that Bruce's bid for power was over, but in 1307, he returned from hiding, allegedly inspired by watching the dogged perseverance of a spider while he sheltered in a cave, and began a campaign of guerrilla warfare against English forces in the north and northeast of Scotland. This was successful, and Bruce defeated both the English and his Comyn enemies in a series of relatively small battles. In July 1307, King Edward I of England died and was replaced by his son, Edward II, a much less effective military leader than his father.

Bruce continued his astutely fought campaign, refusing to meet a large English force in open battle and instead picking off English strongholds and castles in Scotland one by one. By 1314, Bruce's forces not only controlled almost all of Scotland, but he was also mounting raids into northern England. King Edward II responded by raising a very large army, between 15,000-20,000 men and marching north to confront Bruce. In early June, Bruce's troops were besieging one of the last English strongholds in Scotland, Stirling Castle. Edward moved his army north from Berwick to relieve the siege. Bruce with a smaller army of around 6,000 moved to block the English, and the two sides finally met in open battle on June 23, 1314 in the low hills to the south of Stirling near a stream known as the Bannock Burn.

The first day of fighting proved indecisive, though Bruce personally killed one of the leading English knights, Sir Henry de Bohun. The following day, the English attempted once again to march to Stirling. The Scots were waiting to ambush them from thick woodland. The English army was in formations meant for marching, not fighting, and their formidable longbowmen were at the rear of the army where they could not easily be used. The Scottish surprise attack shattered the English army. The survivors fled, and Edward was fortunate to avoid capture. This was a stunning defeat and one from which King Edward II would not recover. He fled first to Berwick and then on to York, giving effective control of Scotland to Bruce—Stirling Castle fell to the Scots soon after.

Defeat at Bannockburn was a crushing blow to the English. With superior tactics, Bruce's guerilla army had routed a much larger and, in theory at least, more formidable foe. In England, many nobles began to question the authority and capability of Edward II.

Next, Robert the Bruce conducted a series of campaigns against England with raids into Yorkshire and Lancashire. He also mounted an invasion of Ireland in an attempt to free that country from English rule. He was even crowned high king of Ireland in 1316, but ultimately he was forced to withdraw and leave it under English rule. In the relative peace that followed, Bruce proved to be as astute at diplomacy as he was as a military leader.

The Declaration of Arbroath in 1320 was a public affirmation of Scotland's right to be recognized as an independent country. In 1324, the Pope, a hugely important figure in the medieval world, recognized Bruce as the legitimate king of Scotland. In 1327, Edward II was deposed in favor of his son, Edward III. In May 1328, further Scottish military action forced Edward III to sign the Treaty of Edinburgh-Northampton. This recognized the independence of Scotland and renounced all English claims on the country. To reinforce the treaty, Bruce's son and heir David married the sister of Edward III.

Robert the Bruce had achieved more than any previous Scottish leader. Scotland was now formally recognized as an independent country. The king was not able to enjoy his success however—by this time, Bruce was very ill indeed. Historians still dispute what precisely afflicted the 54-year-old king. Tuberculosis, syphilis, motor neurone disease, some form of cancer, or a series of strokes have all been suggested. Whatever it was, the effect was debilitating. One person who saw Bruce noted in a letter that "he can scarcely move anything but his tongue."

Robert the Bruce died on June 7, 1329, one month short of his 55th birthday. He left behind a country united, at peace and, virtually for the first time, fully in control of its own destiny. He was succeeded as king of Scots by his eldest son, David, who became King David II and would rule Scotland for more than 40 years.

Yet the struggle to safeguard Scotland from English domination was far from over.

Chapter Five

An Uneasy Peace

"We will and concede for us and all our heirs and successors . . . that the kingdom of Scotland shall remain for ever separate in all respects from the kingdom of England."

—Edward III

By the early 1330s, the main focus for England was not Scotland but France. The French had launched a number of attacks on English ports on the south coast. These were generally small in scale, but many people in England feared a full-scale French invasion. The situation was complicated when Charles IV, the king of France, died in 1328 and left no direct male heir. Edward III was Charles' nephew through his mother, Isabella of France, and was therefore Charles' closest male relative. As far as many English people were concerned, this meant that Edward III was not just the king of England, but also rightfully the next king of France. Perhaps unsurprisingly, the French saw things differently, and in 1328, a first cousin of Charles IV became King Philip VI of France.

Edward seemed to accept this decision, but he remained in control of lands in Aquitaine. As duke of Aquitaine, he was required to pay homage to the king of France, but as he was also king of England, he would not agree to this. This dispute and the series of conflicts between England and France that followed have become known as the Hundred Years' War.

When the son of Robert the Bruce became King David II in 1329, he was just five years old. Once again, a Guardian of Scotland was appointed to rule until he reached the age of majority. The new Guardian was Thomas Randolph, earl of Moray, a Scottish diplomat and soldier who had been one of Bruce's most able and respected supporters. Although the English king was primarily concerned with France, it soon became apparent that he had not forgotten or forgiven the military defeats inflicted on England by the Scots.

Although most people had accepted Robert the Bruce as the legitimate king of Scotland, there was a small faction that maintained that the true king was Edward Balliol, eldest son of the deposed King John. This faction mainly comprised a group of Scottish nobles who had fought with the English during the conflict from 1296-1314. These nobles had been given an ultimatum by Robert the Bruce after the Battle of Bannockburn: either they could return to Scotland within one year and accept his rule, or they would be stripped of their titles and their lands in Scotland. Most refused to accept Bruce as king, and as a result they were deprived of their lands and titles. This group of nobles, led by Edward Balliol and Henry de Beaumont, formerly the earl of Buchan and a talented military leader, became popularly known as "the Disinherited." Edward III rightly saw these men as a possible source of fomenting unrest and rebellion in Scotland against the Guardian appointed to rule in place of young David II.

Then, in July 1332, the Guardian of Scotland died. He had been a respected follower of Bruce and his death after less than three years as Guardian was a major blow to the Scots. He was replaced by Domhnall II, the earl of Mar, on August 2, 1332. Mar would remain in this role for just nine days.

Edward III was still officially at peace with Scotland, but in secret, he was supporting the claim to the Scottish throne being raised by Edward Balliol and the Disinherited. Balliol had amassed a small band of disaffected Scottish ex-nobles, and this group had hired mercenaries. No one is now quite certain how many men Balliol had gathered, but it is not thought to have been more than a few hundred. Despite their small numbers, Balliol and his followers were determined to mount an invasion of Scotland which they hoped would remove David II and see Balliol as the new king.

Edward III was aware of these plans and, though he supported Balliol secretly, he was careful not to openly be seen to provide aid for an insurrection against Scotland and its king as this would constitute a flagrant breach of the Treaty of Edinburgh-Northampton. For this reason, Balliol and his small army were not permitted to launch an attack on Scotland across the River Tweed from English territory. Instead, they were allowed to launch an invasion only if this was done from the sea—if a landing by such a small force can be called an invasion. Edward made it clear that if they failed (which is what he seems to have expected), he would deny all knowledge of them and confiscate any lands they owned in England.

Balliol and the Disinherited set sail from the Humber Estuary in a fleet of small ships and landed near Kinghorn in Fife (where King Alexander III had died in 1286) on August 6, 1332. The question of Scottish independence was about to explode into open warfare once again.

Chapter Six

The Pretender to the Throne

"Scotland is not wholly surrounded by sea, unfortunately."

—Grieve

Edward Balliol and his small force of mercenaries set off from Kinghorn in Fife and began a march towards the city of Perth. They were quickly met by a much larger force of Scottish troops under the command of the new Guardian of Scotland, the earl of Mar. The balance of forces was clearly massively in favor of Mar. However, Balliol's army was led by Henry de Beaumont, and it was soon clear that he had learned a great deal during his exile in England.

The two forces met at the River Earn, a few miles from Perth. Mar commanded an army of around 10,000-15,000 men. The precise size of Edward Balliol's army is not known with certainty, but it is believed to have comprised around 1,500 men. The infantry comprised large numbers of longbowmen. The earl of Mar arranged his army in tight formations. Henry de Beaumont arranged a screen of dismounted men-at-arms protecting the mass of archers. During the battle that followed, just as at the Battle of Falkirk at which William Wallace had been defeated in 1298, these longbowmen released a deadly hail of arrows which caused carnage amongst the packed formations facing them.

The outcome of what has become known as the Battle of Dupplin Moor was a rout for forces loyal to King David. Casualties are not known with certainty, but it is believed that Balliol's army suffered merely 33 men killed. Mar's army suffered casualties that have been estimated at anything between 2,000 and 10,000. Worse still, the new Guardian of Scotland was himself killed during the battle, just nine days after his election. Other casualties included Robert Bruce (an illegitimate son of Robert the Bruce), Thomas Randolph, earl of Moray, Murdoch III, earl of Menteith, and Alexander Fraser, the high chamberlain of Scotland.

This defeat was a stunning reversal for those loyal to King David. The earl of Dunbar was in command of another army, almost as large as that of the earl of Mar. This was positioned behind Balliol's army, between it and the coast. Dunbar, however, seemed so disheartened by the defeat of Mar that he did not even attempt to attack Balliol's force.

Balliol marched on to Perth, and in September 1332, he was crowned king of Scotland. It was soon apparent that the new king did not have popular support in Scotland, and he was forced to move to a safer area at Annan in the south of Scotland close to the English border. Even there and surrounded by his supporters, Balliol was not safe. On December 16, just three months after his coronation, the new king was forced to flee to England when supporters of King David attacked the house in which he was staying.

Balliol immediately appealed to Edward III for help. He pledged to recognize Edward as his liege and offered the English king lands in Scotland, including the city of Berwick, in return for his support. Edward was quick to recognize this fortuitous and completely unexpected opportunity. He claimed that the Treaty of Edinburgh-Northampton had been broken by the Scots who had pursued Balliol across the border, and he pledged support for Edward Balliol as the rightful king of Scotland.

Meanwhile, another Guardian of Scotland had come and gone. The earl of Mar was replaced by Sir Andrew Murray. He was captured during fighting at Roxburgh between supporters of Balliol and King David and taken to England. His successor was Sir Archibald Douglas, one of those who had led the attack on Balliol's house in Annan.

In April 1333, Edward Balliol returned to Scotland with a small army and laid siege to the city of Berwick. An army under the command of Sir Archibald Douglas attacked, and Edward III used this as a justification for sending an English army into Scotland to support Balliol. In July 1333, the combined forces of Edward and Balliol faced a loyalist Scottish army at the Battle of Halidon Hill. Once again, the English longbowmen proved decisive; the loyalist army was defeated and Sir Archibald Douglas was killed. The loss of yet another Guardian of Scotland in such a short time was a major blow to the supporters of David, and the young king was taken to France in order to assure his safety.

Balliol was confirmed as king of Scotland, and he quickly pledged allegiance to Edward III and ceded the city of Berwick to England. Pressure from Edward forced

Balliol to cede more Scottish cities in the south to the English king later that year. These included Roxburgh, Edinburgh, Peebles, Dumfries, and Haddington until the English were in control of large areas of the south of Scotland.

Balliol was still not able to generate any large-scale support in Scotland. With the aid of the English, he controlled parts of the borders and the south of Scotland, but in the Highlands, the Western Isles, and the northeast, there was still substantial support for the deposed and exiled King David II. Balliol was further weakened by disputes amongst his own supporters who squabbled over what they saw as their rightful rewards for their service and continuing defections amongst his troops; increasing numbers were going over to the loyalist side.

In the winter of 1334/1335 and for his own safety, Balliol was forced to retreat to Berwick, now an English city.

Chapter Seven

Return of the King

"Seeing Scotland is only seeing a worse England."

—James Boswell

The relationship between England and France was becoming increasingly tense, and Edward III was less than delighted when he returned from a trip to Scotland to find waiting for him the bishop of Avranches, sent to London by King Philip VI to try to broker a deal between Scotland and England which would see the reinstatement of the deposed King David, who was still in France. Nothing came of this but, by early 1335, Balliol's grip on Scotland was looking increasingly tenuous.

Scottish ships were regularly attacking ships traveling from England with supplies for his troops. The estates occupied by two of his main supporters were attacked and occupied by loyalists. By March 1335, Edward III decided that he would have to intervene directly to protect his ally Balliol. He gathered an army of 13,000 men, the largest army he had taken to Scotland, and in July, he marched north.

The loyalists, who had been squabbling amongst themselves, were united by the new English invasion. Still, much of the Lowlands of Scotland was quickly occupied by the English. Philip VI responded by raising an army of

6,000 men and threatening to send this to Scotland unless Edward agreed to accept the arbitration of the Pope on the question of Scotland. Edward refused, though his army was unable to make much progress beyond the Lowlands.

In 1336, the military situation was becoming more serious for Edward III. The threat of a French army landing in Scotland seemed very real, and this would leave England vulnerable to an attack from the north. He moved north once again and sacked several Scottish cities including Aberdeen in the northeast, the most likely point for a French landing. The situation in Scotland was grave, with famine and disease major factors, but the loyalists continued to fight a mainly guerrilla war under the command of Sir Andrew Murray who had been reinstated as Guardian of Scotland after being released from captivity by the English.

It was only the threat of a French invasion that finally stopped Edward's campaign in Scotland, and he returned to England in December 1336 to begin planning for an English invasion of Gascony. The loyalists took advantage of the wavering interest of Edward in the campaign in Scotland to increase the level of their attacks, and by March 1336, they were in control of virtually all of Scotland north of the River Forth.

By 1337, the loyalist side, provided with ample supplies by France, had extended its control over Scotland to the extent that it was mounting small-scale raids across the border and into northern England. Still distracted by the imminent war against France, Edward sent William Montagu, the 1st earl of Salisbury, to Scotland to take charge of the war there. In January 1338, Salisbury led an

English army against the fortress of Dunbar, but after six months of effort, he had achieved very little, and Edward recalled him.

By the winter of 1338, the loyalists controlled virtually all of Scotland, leaving Balliol with only small areas close to the cities of Perth and Cupar. Then, the loyalist campaign suffered a blow with the death of Sir Andrew Murray. He was replaced as Guardian by Robert Stewart, the former high chamberlain of Scotland and the heir to the throne after David. Under Stewart's leadership, the loyalists took control of the last remaining areas of Scotland, and Balliol was once again forced to retreat to Berwick.

In June 1341, King David II, now 17 years of age, returned to Scotland to reclaim his throne. One of his main tasks was to unite his followers, who were increasingly beginning to fight amongst themselves now that the immediate threat of an English invasion had been removed. At one point, one of the senior loyalist leaders had another starved to death in his castle because he was jealous of rewards the other man had been given for military successes.

By this time, hostility between England and France had exploded into open war. Starting with a naval engagement in the Battle of Sluys in 1340 in which the French lost more than 15,000 men, the conflict was not going well for France. By 1343, France had lost several important cities to the English, and it was only the direct intervention of the Pope who brokered a peace deal that brought the war to a temporary end. This deal also included Scotland, and so for a short time, the ongoing conflict between Scotland and

England was reduced to no more than a series of small skirmishes across the border.

In June 1346, the brief peace between France and England ended when Edward arrived on the Cotentin peninsula of Normandy with an army of 10,000 men. In August that year, the French and English armies met in open battle for the first time at the Battle of Crécy. Just as they had against the Scots, the English longbowmen proved lethal, and the French suffered a catastrophic defeat, losing as many as 15,000 men in a single day. Panicked by this, the French king appealed to Scotland to relieve pressure while the French reorganized and mounted an invasion of English territory in France.

King David agreed, and in September 1346, he gathered a large army and crossed the border into England. Initially, the invasion of England went well, partly because Edward III and the bulk of the English army was in France, preparing to besiege the strategically vital port city of Calais. In October, the Scottish army had advanced as far south as the city of Durham and met English forces at the Battle of Neville's Cross near the city of Durham, south of Newcastle. The Scottish army was considerably larger, around 12,000 men facing an English army of 7,000. However, the outcome was a humiliating defeat for the Scots. They surrendered, and King David, wounded during the battle, fled only to be captured soon after.

The surviving Scots retreated back over the border where they were followed by the victorious English who were once again able to occupy much of the south of Scotland. David was taken to the Tower of London where he was held as a prisoner. In France, Calais finally fell to the English after a protracted siege. The fortunes of the Scots and their French allies were at a low point.

Chapter Eight

The End of the Wars

"The best-laid schemes of mice and men often go astray."

—Robert Burns

Following the loyalist defeat at the Battle of Neville's Cross, Edward Balliol and his supporters returned to Scotland where they occupied parts of the Lowlands and backed an insurrection in Galloway. Just as before, however, Balliol found little popular support in Scotland, and most of those who followed him were interested more in the possibility of loot and plunder than reinstating Balliol as king.

It looked as if there was little to stop England once again occupying Scotland when a completely new and unexpected factor appeared—the Black Death. This devastating pandemic would lead to the deaths of an estimated 75-200 million people in Eurasia. The plague first reached England in 1348, and by September, London and large parts of the south and south east of England were being ravaged by the disease. Scotland remained relatively free from the disease until, in 1349, the Scots took advantage of the devastating effects of the plague on England to launch another invasion which once again reached as far south as the city of Durham.

However, though the Scottish invasion was briefly successful, it wasn't long before its troops began to succumb to the deadly disease. When they returned home, they brought the Black Death with them, and by 1350, large parts of Scotland were being devastated by the plague. A contemporary chronicler noted: "In 1350, there was a great pestilence and mortality of men in the kingdom of Scotland. So great a plague has never been heard of from the beginning of the world to the present day, or been recorded in books."

France was also badly affected, and the fighting in Normandy virtually stopped as both the French and English armies were ravaged by disease. The conflict in Normandy descended into a stalemate with neither side being strong enough to directly challenge or defeat the other.

In the absence of King David and despite the Black Death, Scottish forces rallied under the leadership of Robert Stewart. By this time it was becoming apparent that Edward III was intent on focusing on the war with France and wanted to bring the conflict with Scotland to an end. His first offer to the imprisoned King David was that he would be released if he agreed to recognize Scotland as England's fiefdom and agree that, if he should die without a direct heir, the throne of Scotland would pass to Edward III or his son. This was refused, but it was notable that neither this nor any subsequent offer from the English king made any mention of Balliol. It seemed that Edward III had finally recognized that Balliol would never be accepted as king by the vast majority of Scots.

Two years later, Edward made a second offer: he would release David on the payment of a large ransom and on the condition that Edward's son, John of Gaunt, was named as heir to the Scottish throne in the event that Davis died without producing a child. David seemed inclined to accept this offer, and in early 1352, he was briefly released from captivity to return to Scotland to try to persuade Parliament to accept. He faced a major source of opposition in the form of Robert Stewart and his supporters. Stewart was still formally the heir to the Scottish throne after David, and he and his supporters were not interested in signing a deal that would nullify this. The Scottish Parliament rejected the offer in March of 1352, and David was sent back into captivity in England.

In 1354, Edward made his final offer: the payment of a simple ransom for the release of David with no claim on the Scottish throne. This too was refused, partly because negotiations were in hand to seal a more binding alliance with France. In 1355, with supplies and equipment provided by France, a Scottish army which included a number of French knights was assembled for an invasion of England and what would prove to be the final series of battles in the Wars of Scottish Independence.

At the Battle of Nesbit Moor, the Scots won a decisive victory against a small English army, and next, they laid siege on the hapless city of Berwick which was quickly burned and sacked. Their timing, however, was bad. The war with France was in another brief period of hiatus and Edward III was able to give his full attention to Scotland and to bring to bear the bulk of his army against the Scots.

In early 1356, Edward advanced into Scotland once more. This time, his intention was not occupation. An increasingly common element of the war against France had become *chevauchées,* raids intended to intimidate the enemy by killing civilians and destroying infrastructure, mills, farms, and villages, therefore making the countryside as unproductive as possible for the enemy. When Edward's army swept into Scotland in late January of 1356, his intention was to cause as much destruction and terror as possible in as short a time as possible. For a month, his troops ravaged Lothian, burning the city of Edinburgh, the town of Haddington, and many smaller towns and villages. This event was to become known to the Scots as "Burnt Candlemas."

One of the people who followed in the wake of Edward's army was Edward Balliol, but by this time he had become a marginal figure. In January, he agreed to give up his claim on the Scottish throne in exchange for a generous pension from Edward III. He retired to live in obscurity in the north of England and died childless in 1367.

The effects of continuing wars and the ravages of the Black Death had left Scotland impoverished and weak. Burnt Candlemas was, for many people, the final horror. Suddenly, many Scots seemed as keen as the English king to bring the series of conflicts to an end. The situation was made worse because Scotland's ally France was faring badly in its war with England. In September 1356, the French had suffered another massive military defeat at the Battle of Poitiers, and the French king, John II, was captured and joined David in captivity in London. French defeats meant that little support could be expected from that quarter for any further Scottish wars with England.

In 1357, the Wars of Scottish Independence were formally brought to an end by the signing of the Treaty of

Berwick. Under this treaty, the Scots agreed to pay a large ransom for the release of David. This was to be paid in several installments for the simple reason that the Scottish government did not have the money to make a single payment. Edward III was happy—the treaty left him free to concentrate on the war with France and the ransom would help to fund that war. In addition, the important city of Berwick would finally become officially English.

When the treaty was signed, King David II was released and returned to Scotland.

Chapter Nine

Aftermath

"To a Scot, the past clings like sand to wet feet, and is carried about as a burden."

—Geddes MacGregor

The Treaty of Berwick is generally taken by historians to mark the end of the Wars of Scottish Independence and the beginning of true Scottish independence. However, it did not bring an end to wars between Scotland and England. Skirmishes continued until the eighteenth century when another war ended with Scotland finally accepting English rule and becoming part of the United Kingdom.

King David II ruled an impoverished Scotland on his return. The large ransom payments were scheduled to be made in ten annual installments. The first payment was made on time, the second was late, and Scotland was never able to raise sufficient funds to make a third. In 1363, David traveled to London and made an offer to Edward III that, if he was willing to forget about the ransom, David would name the English king or one of his sons as heir to the Scottish throne. It seems certain that the Scottish Parliament would have rejected such a deal and it was never formalized, but it seemed to distract Edward's attention and no further ransom payments were made by the Scots.

David II died in 1371 at the age of 46. He left no children, and his successor as king of Scots was Robert Stewart who was crowned Robert II in February of 1371. David was the last Scottish king from the House of Bruce, and from 1371 until the union with England, all future Scottish kings would come from the House of Stewart.

King Edward III died in 1377, still pursuing his war against France which would not finally end until 1453 with the almost complete ejection of English forces from mainland Europe. Edward was succeeded by his ten-year-old son, Richard II, who proved to be a much less determined and focused leader than his father; his personality issues became so great that he was deposed in 1399.

Conclusion

The first phase of the Wars of Scottish Independence, from 1296-1328, has become known as the First War of Scottish Independence and produced clear-cut military victories and saw the emergence of two men who have become national heroes in Scotland: William Wallace and Robert the Bruce. The second phase, from 1332-1357, which culminated in the Treaty of Berwick, has become known as the Second War of Scottish Independence but is much more difficult to follow, and it is only recently that historians have classified this series of conflicts as being part of a single war.

The border between Scotland and England is still almost precisely as it was agreed in 1357, and Berwick-upon-Tweed, which changed hands so many times during these wars, remains English though many of its inhabitants still feel an affinity for Scotland. Scottish independence effectively ended with the Act of Union of 1707 under which Scotland became part of the United Kingdom of Great Britain, ruled by a Parliament in London. This was reversed to an extent by the Devolution Referendum of 1997 in which Scotland voted for the creation of a devolved Scottish Parliament which was established in 1999. Many Scots still wish to see complete independence from the United Kingdom, and figures from the Wars of Scottish Independence, such as Wallace and Bruce, are used as icons by this movement.

The Auld Alliance created during these wars is still remembered fondly in both countries, and there is an affection between France and Scotland which is generally not shared by other parts of the United Kingdom.

The Wars of Scottish Independence ended not with a great victory for either side but with a weariness for war brought about by 60 years of intermittent conflict. The Treaty of Berwick did not really solve the issue of whether Scotland could be truly independent from England, though it brought more than 200 years of self-government for Scotland. Though the last battle happened more than 600 years ago, the Wars of Scottish Independence still cast a shadow over the relationship between the two countries.

Made in the USA
Middletown, DE
31 December 2023

47024752R00027